Posters, Prompts, and Graphic Organizers That Make Writing Practice Fun!

- **Story writing**
- **Personal narratives**
- **Descriptive writing**
- **Informational writing**

Choose a different poster each week of the school year!

Managing Editor: Gerri Primak

Editorial Team: Becky S. Andrews, Diane Badden, Kimberley Bruck, Karen A. Brudnak, Kitty Campbell, Jenny Chapman, Chris Curry, Lynette Dickerson, Lynn Drolet, Theresa Lewis Goode, Tazmen Hansen, Marsha Heim, Lori Z. Henry, Debra Liverman, Dorothy C. McKinney, Thad H. McLaurin, Laura Mihalenko, Sharon Murphy, Jennifer Nunn, Mark Rainey, Hope Rodgers, Eliseo De Jesus Santos II, Rebecca Saunders, Barry Slate, Zane Williard

www.themailbox.com

Manufactured in the United States
10 9 8 7 6 5 4 3 2 1

TABLE OF CONTENTS

STORY WRITING

PERSONAL NARRATIVE

DESCRIPTIVE WRITING

INFORMATIONAL WRITING

WHAT'S INSIDE

38
pull-out mini posters with **word banks** and **writing prompts**

All Dressed Up

Write a paragraph that shares information about your wardrobe.
Read the word bank. Choose a main idea.
Be sure to include details that support your main idea.

Main Ideas
- Getting Dressed for School
- Getting Dressed for a Fancy Party
- Getting Dressed for a Sports Game

Word Bank

hand-me-down	tattered
brand-new	favorite
unusual	stylish
wear	popular
rags	plaid

38
prewriting organizers

Informational Writing
Main idea and details

Name _____

Main idea:

Plan the details in your paragraph that support the main idea.

Detail:

Detail:

Detail:

Word Bank

hand-me-down	unusual	rags	favorite	popular
brand-new	wear	tattered	stylish	plaid

WRITING CHECKLIST

Author _____

Date _____

Check all that apply.

Ideas	☐ easy to understand ☐ good supporting details
Organization	☐ beginning ☐ middle ☐ end
Voice	☐ engaging ☐ purposeful
Sentences	☐ complete ☐ good variety ☐ easy to read
Conventions	☐ correct spelling ☐ correct punctuation ☐ correct capitalization ☐ correct grammar
Presentation	☐ neat

Checklist completed by

_____

Instant Writing • ©The Mailbox® Books • TEC61162

WRITING CHECKLIST

Author _____

Date _____

Check all that apply.

Ideas	☐ easy to understand ☐ good supporting details
Organization	☐ beginning ☐ middle ☐ end
Voice	☐ engaging ☐ purposeful
Sentences	☐ complete ☐ good variety ☐ easy to read
Conventions	☐ correct spelling ☐ correct punctuation ☐ correct capitalization ☐ correct grammar
Presentation	☐ neat

Checklist completed by

_____

Instant Writing • ©The Mailbox® Books • TEC61162

Note to the teacher: Use the checklist to evaluate a student's writing, or ask a student to use the checklist to evaluate his own writing.

What a Wacky Classroom!

Write a story about a strange classroom.
Read the word bank. Choose a story starter.

Word Bank

school	funny
crazy	teacher
different	lesson
unusual	surprise
juggle	laugh

Story Starters

- This morning, when I walked in my classroom…

- This is going to be a very strange year!

- You'll never guess what we did in school today!

Story writing

Story starter:

List ideas to help plan your story about the strange classroom.

In a Real Classroom	In an Imaginary Classroom

Word Bank

school	funny
crazy	teacher
different	lesson
unusual	surprise
juggle	laugh

Instant Writing • ©The Mailbox® Books • TEC61162

6   **Note to the teacher:** Use with "What a Wacky Classroom!" on page 5.

A Fetching Tale

Write a story about a hat-catching dog.
Read the word bank. Choose a story starter.
Describe your story's setting, characters, and events.

Word Bank

high	throw	bone
leap	award	clothes
talent	snatch	punish
	skill	

Story Starters

- My dog is really confused.

- Mr. Brown's dog always gets into trouble.

- There are some unusual new events at this year's dog show.

Rover

Story starter:

Plan your story about a hat-catching dog.

Characters

Setting

Events

Word Bank

high	talent	award	skill	clothes
leap	throw	snatch	bone	punish

Instant Writing • ©The Mailbox® Books • TEC61162

Note to the teacher: Use with "A Fetching Tale" on page 7.

What a Trip!

Write a letter to a friend telling a story of a pretend vacation you took.
Read the word bank. Choose a topic.
Make sure your story has a main idea and details.

Topics

- My Awesome Vacation
- My weirdest vacation was…
- If only you had been there!

Word Bank

plane	visit	camera
cruise	relax	suitcase
train	exciting	backpack
	sights	

Topic:

Plan your letter telling the story of a pretend vacation.

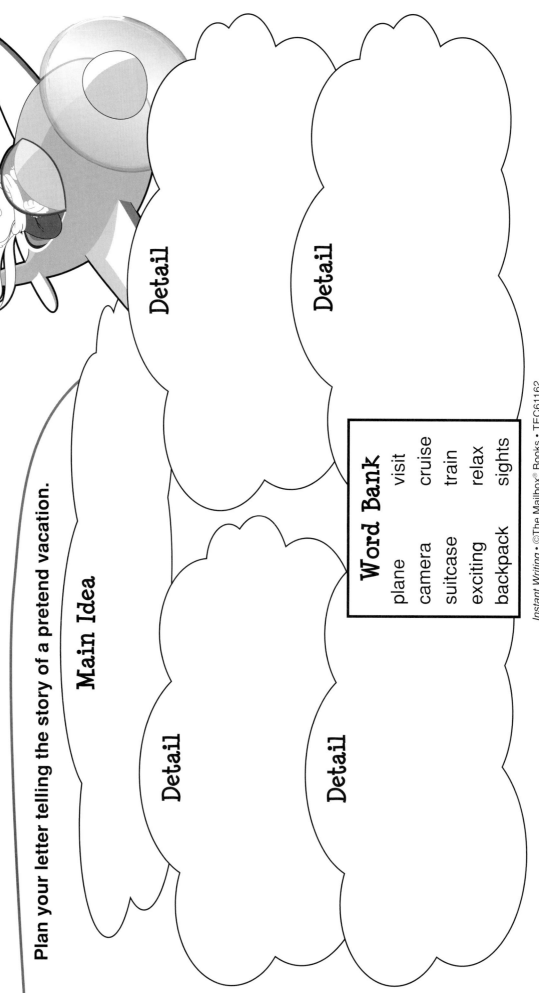

Main Idea

Detail

Detail

Detail

Detail

Word Bank

plane	visit
camera	cruise
suitcase	train
exciting	relax
backpack	sights

Note to the teacher: Use with "What a Trip!" on page 9.

A Fantastic Find!

Write a story about finding a magic bottle.
Read the word bank. Choose a topic.
Make sure your story has a main idea and details.

Word Bank

poof	wish
genie	surprise
magic	dirty
scared	confused
helpful	dream

Topics

- The Bottle I Found

- My Three Wishes

- Genie in the Bottle

Topic:

Plan your story about finding a magic bottle.

Main Idea:

Detail:

Detail:

Detail:

Word Bank

| poof | wish | genie | surprise | magic |
| dirty | confused | dream | scared | helpful |

Instant Writing • ©The Mailbox® Books • TEC61162

12   **Note to the teacher:** Use with "A Fantastic Find!" on page 11.

A Colorful Snack

Write a story about a kite-eating giraffe.
Read the word bank. Choose a story starter.
Make sure your story has a beginning,
a middle, and an end.

Word Bank

swallow	surprise	crunch
gust	tangle	chew
reach	stretch	grab
delicious		

Story Starters

- Last night, I had the strangest dream.

- My trip to the zoo was full of surprises!

- The zookeeper stopped, stared, and shook his head.

Story writing

Story starter:

Plan your story about the kite-eating giraffe.

Beginning:

Middle:

End:

Word Bank

swallow	surprise	crunch	gust	tangle
chew	reach	stretch	grab	delicious

Instant Writing • ©The Mailbox® Books • TEC61162

14   **Note to the teacher:** Use with "A Colorful Snack" on page 13.

Ticktock

Write a story about an unusual clock.
Read the word bank. Choose a story starter.
Make sure your story has a beginning,
a middle, and an end.

Word Bank

hour   roar
chime   hands
wooden   midnight
pendulum   cock-a-doodle-doo
startle   funny

Story Starters

- Last night, our cuckoo clock did something strange.

- I knew we should have bought a different clock!

- My grandmother's clock is one of a kind.

- Our new clock gives me a headache.

Story starter:

Plan your story about an unusual clock.

Beginning

Middle

End

Word Bank

hour	roar	chime	hands	wooden
midnight	pendulum	cock-a-doodle-doo	startle	funny

Instant Writing • ©The Mailbox® Books • TEC61162

Pouch Surprise!

Write a story about a surprised kangaroo.
Read the word bank. Choose a topic.
Make sure your story has a beginning, a middle, and an end.

Word Bank

hidden	secret
deep	dark
escaped	lost
unexpected	worry
tickle	heavy

Topics

- The kangaroo was shocked when she looked in her pouch.

- The kangaroo didn't realize she had a hole in her pouch.

- The baby porcupine thought he had found the perfect hiding place.

Story writing

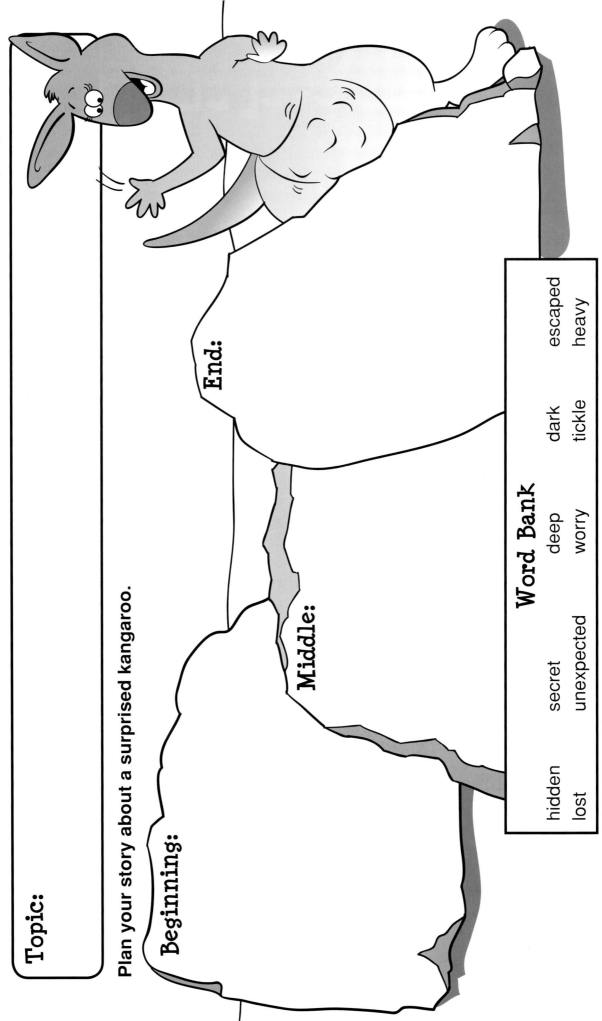

Topic:

Plan your story about a surprised kangaroo.

Beginning:

Middle:

End:

Word Bank

| hidden | secret | deep | dark | escaped |
| lost | unexpected | worry | tickle | heavy |

Instant Writing • ©The Mailbox® Books • TEC61162

Note to the teacher: Use with "Pouch Surprise!" on page 17.

Topsy-turvy!

Write a story about an
  upside-down day.
Read the word bank. Choose
  a story starter.
Be sure to tell the story in the
  order that it happens.

Word Bank

upside-down

dizzy

grip

weird

difficult

unusual

confused

covered

disappear

invisible

Story Starters

- When I woke up this morning, I knew
  something was wrong.

- When I looked in the mirror…

- I started feeling dizzy when…

Story writing

Story starter:

Plan your story about an upside-down day.

First...

| Then... |

| Next... |

| Finally,... |

Word Bank

upside-down	dizzy	grip	weird	difficult
unusual	confused	covered	disappear	invisible

Instant Writing • ©The Mailbox® Books • TEC61162

20 **Note to the teacher:** Use with "Topsy-turvy!" on page 19.

The Candy Factory

Write a story about working in a candy factory.
Read the word bank.
Choose a topic.
Use your senses to add details to your story.

Word Bank

delicious	sweet
loud	gooey
noisy	sticky
yummy	chocolate
melt	fast

Topics

- My Day at the Candy Factory
- I invented a new kind of candy!
- The Super Speedy Candy Machine

Name _____

Topic: _____

Write details about working in a candy factory.

Sights

Tastes

Sounds

Feelings

Smells

Word Bank

| delicious | sweet | loud | gooey | noisy |
| sticky | yummy | chocolate | melt | fast |

Instant Writing • ©The Mailbox® Books • TEC61162

Note to the teacher: Use with "The Candy Factory" on page 21.

What Is It?

Write a letter to a friend telling a story about an imaginary animal.
Read the word bank. Choose a topic.
Use lots of describing words in your letter.

CAUTION: MYSTERY ANIMAL INSIDE

Word Bank

tremendous   swim
tiny   leap
strange   dangerous
cage   friendly
exciting   surprise

Topics

- My New and Unusual Pet

- On my way to school, I saw…

- The New Zoo Exhibit

Story writing

Name_____

Topic:

Plan your letter telling the story about an imaginary animal.

It looks like:

It sounds like:

It feels like:

Word Bank

| tremendous | cage | dangerous | tiny | exciting |
| friendly | strange | swim | surprise | leap |

Instant Writing • ©The Mailbox® Books • TEC61162

24 **Note to the teacher:** Use with "What Is It?" on page 23.

Knock! Knock!

Write a story about who is at the door.
Read the word bank. Choose a topic.
Use lots of describing words in your story.

Word Bank

creepy	afraid
doorbell	arrived
friendly	confused
polite	unusual
slimy	enormous

Topics

- My best friend loves to play tricks on me.

- Last night, we had an unexpected visitor.

- Our New Neighbor

Write descriptive words and phrases to plan your story about who is at the door.

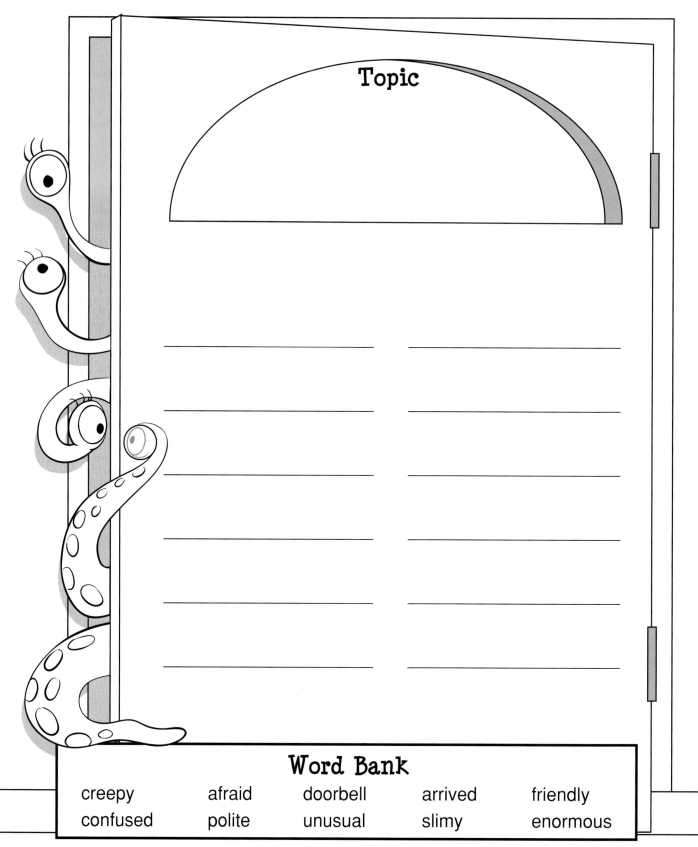

Topic

Word Bank

creepy	afraid	doorbell	arrived	friendly
confused	polite	unusual	slimy	enormous

Instant Writing • ©The Mailbox® Books • TEC61162

26   **Note to the teacher:** Use with "Knock! Knock!" on page 25.

On the Road Again

Write a paragraph about a trip you have taken.
Read the word bank. Choose a topic.
Be sure to answer the following questions:
Who? What? When? Where? Why?

Topics

- The Best Trip I've Taken
- The Worst Trip I've Taken
- The Funniest Trip I've Taken

Word Bank

hotel	visit
vacation	suitcase
travel	favorite
fantastic	weather
unforgettable	excitement

Personal narrative

Topic:

Answer each question to help you organize a retelling of the trip.

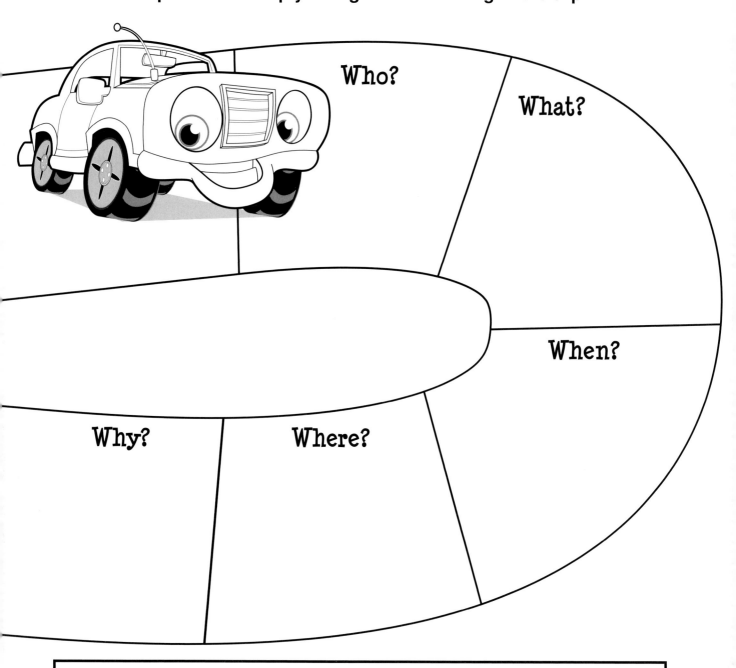

Who?

What?

When?

Why?

Where?

Word Bank

hotel	vacation	travel	fantastic	unforgettable
visit	suitcase	favorite	weather	excitement

Friendship

Write a story to retell an event shared with a friend.
Read the word bank. Choose a story starter.
Make sure your story includes how you felt about
the time spent together.

Story Starters

- I'll never forget the time when...
- The funniest thing my friend and I did...
- The time I went to the movies with...

Word Bank

funny

entertaining

together

noisy

enjoyable

laugh

incredible

munchies

snacks

exciting

Personal narrative

Story starter:

Plan your story to retell an event shared with a friend.

Who?

Where?

When?

What?

How did you feel?

Word Bank

exciting	incredible	munchies	snacks	enjoyable
together	entertaining	funny	laugh	noisy

Instant Writing • ©The Mailbox® Books • TEC61162

30   **Note to the teacher:** Use with "Friendship" on page 29.

Great Big Thanks!

Thank You!

Write a thank-you note.
Read the word bank. Choose a topic.
Think about who you are writing to and decide what you want the person to know.

Topics

- Thank a family member for a special gift.
- Thank a parent for something that was done for you.
- Thank a friend for being a great pal.

Word Bank

appreciate
considerate
beautiful
thoughtful
thankful

enjoy
surprise
special
care
receive

Personal narrative
Audience and purpose

Topic

Plan your thank-you note.

What do you want your audience to know?

Who is your audience?

Word Bank

appreciate	thoughtful	enjoy
considerate	thankful	surprise
beautiful		special
		care
		receive

Instant Writing • ©The Mailbox® Books • TEC61162

Note to the teacher: Use with "Great Big Thanks!" on page 31.

Tidying Up

Write a letter telling how you feel about cleaning responsibilities.
Read the word bank. Choose a topic.
Think about who you are writing to and decide what you want the person to know.

Instant Writing • ©The Mailbox® Books • TEC61162

Topics

- I Appreciate Cleanliness
- I'm Messy!
- Why I Like or Dislike My Chores

Word Bank

allowance	chore
refreshing	sudsy
stinky	wrinkly
clean	tired
dusty	blisters

Personal narrative
Audience and purpose

Topic:

Answer each question to help you plan your letter about cleaning responsibilities.

I will write to...

What do you want your audience to know?

Word Bank

allowance	stinky	dusty	sudsy	tired
refreshing	clean	chore	wrinkly	blisters

Note to the teacher: Use with "Tidying Up" on page 33.

Say Cheese, Please!

Write a paragraph about a time when you had your
   picture taken.
Read the word bank. Choose a main idea.
Use details to support the main idea in your writing.

Word Bank

pose
smile
avoid
album
school
family
camera
photographer
scrapbook
embarrassing

Main Ideas

- My Favorite Photograph

- I wish that picture was never taken!

- My most embarrassing picture ever…

Personal narrative

Personal narrative

Main idea and details

Main idea:

List details to support the main idea in your paragraph.

Word Bank

pose	family
smile	camera
avoid	photographer
album	scrapbook
school	embarrassing

Instant Writing • ©The Mailbox® Books • TEC61162

Note to the teacher: Use with "Say Cheese, Please!" on page 35.

My Family

Write a paragraph that tells about your family.
Read the word bank. Choose a main idea.
Make sure your paragraph uses details to support
the main idea in your writing.

Instant Writing • ©The Mailbox® Books • TEC61162

Word Bank

love
sharing
siblings
disagree
related
memories
laughter
heartfelt
remember
unique

Main Ideas

- Everyone in my family is special.
- When my family gets together,
  there's a lot to talk about!
- I enjoy my family's traditions.

Personal narrative

Personal narrative

Main idea and details

Main idea: _____

List details to help you write a paragraph about your family.

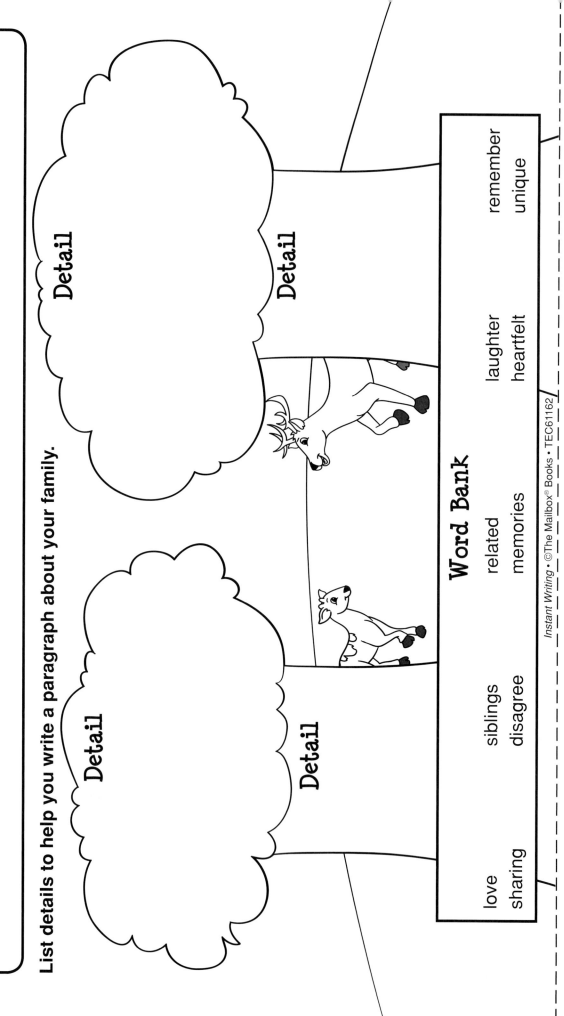

Detail

Detail

Detail

Detail

Word Bank

love	related	laughter	remember
sharing	memories	heartfelt	unique
siblings			
disagree			

Note to the teacher: Use with "My Family" on page 37.

Tapping Tunes

Write an essay to share your experiences and ideas about music.
Read the word bank. Choose a main idea.
Make sure your essay uses details to support your main idea.

Main Ideas

- Loud music is the best kind.
- Music makes me feel happy.
- Music is overrated.
- I can listen to music all day long.

The Crustacean Station Band

Word Bank

relaxing	melody	exercise	instrument
energizing	volume	popular	orchestra
soothing	sound		

Personal narrative

Main idea: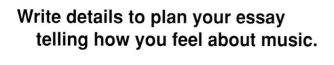

Write details to plan your essay
telling how you feel about music.

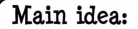

Detail:

Detail:

Detail:

Word Bank

| relaxing | soothing | volume | exercise | instrument |
| energizing | melody | sound | popular | orchestra |

Instant Writing • ©The Mailbox® Books • TEC61162

An Act of Kindness

Instant Writing • ©The Mailbox® Books • TEC61162

Word Bank

considerate	emergency
incredible	begged
frustrated	special
appreciated	heartfelt
thankful	desperate

Write a paragraph about a time when you acted kindly.

Read the word bank. Choose a topic.

Make sure your story has a beginning, a middle, and an end.

Story Starters

• My friend was so thankful when I helped....

• I really like to help....

• One time when I tried to help someone, it didn't work.

Personal narrative

42

Story starter:

Plan your paragraph about a time when you acted kindly.

Beginning

Middle

End

Word Bank

| considerate | thankful | special | appreciated | heartfelt |
| frustrated | emergency | incredible | begged | desperate |

Instant Writing • ©The Mailbox® Books • TEC61162

Note to the teacher: Use with "An Act of Kindness" on page 41.

My Busy Morning

Write a story that tells what you do when you get ready for school. Read the word bank. Choose a topic. Be sure to plan the sequence of your story.

Word Bank

snooze
rush
quickly
grab
breakfast

toothbrush
backpack
sign
planner
homework

Story Starters

- As soon as the alarm goes off, I...
- After I roll out of bed, I...
- The best way to start my morning is...

Personal narrative

Personal narrative
Sequencing events

Story starter:

Write the steps you take when getting ready for school to help you organize your story.

First:

Next:

Then:

Finally:

Word Bank

snooze	breakfast	backpack	planner
quickly	toothbrush	sign	homework
rush	grab		

Note to the teacher: Use with "My Busy Morning" on page 43.

What a Sport!

Write a poem that expresses your ideas about sports.
Read the word bank. Choose a topic.
Be sure to include lots of descriptive words or phrases.

Word Bank

active	challenge	practice
healthy	training	sweaty
exercise	compete	energy
	lazy	

Topics

- A Sensational Sport
- Fast and Furious
- Sports Are Not for Me!

Personal narrative

Topic:

Write descriptive phrases to plan your poem about your feelings about sports.

Word Bank

| challenge | lazy | active | exercise | practice |
| sweaty | healthy | training | compete | energy |

Instant Writing • ©The Mailbox® Books • TEC61162

46   **Note to the teacher:** Use with "What a Sport!" on page 45.

Check It Out!

Write a descriptive paragraph about an unexpected find.
Read the word bank. Choose a topic.
Be sure to use your imagination to visualize what was found
    before you write.

Topics

- A New Bug in the Garden

- A Fossil in the Backyard

- A Treasure on the Beach

Word Bank

hairy	wet
smooth	old
fuzzy	unknown
prickly	excited
cold	surprised

Descriptive writing

Topic: _____

Plan a descriptive paragraph about the unexpected find.

Draw in the wagon what
was found.

Size and shape:

Feels like:

I felt...

Word Bank				
hairy	unknown	smooth	prickly	wet
fuzzy	cold	old	surprised	excited

Instant Writing • ©The Mailbox® Books • TEC61162

48   **Note to the teacher:** Use with "Check It Out!" on page 47.

What's Cooking?

Write a letter describing a meal you ate.
Read the word bank. Choose an audience.
Be sure to describe what you liked and
disliked about the meal.

Word Bank

tasty	sweet	dry
ingredients	sour	slimy
spicy	recipe	salty
	delicious	

Audience Options

- Food Critic
- Family Member
- School Cafeteria Worker

Descriptive writing

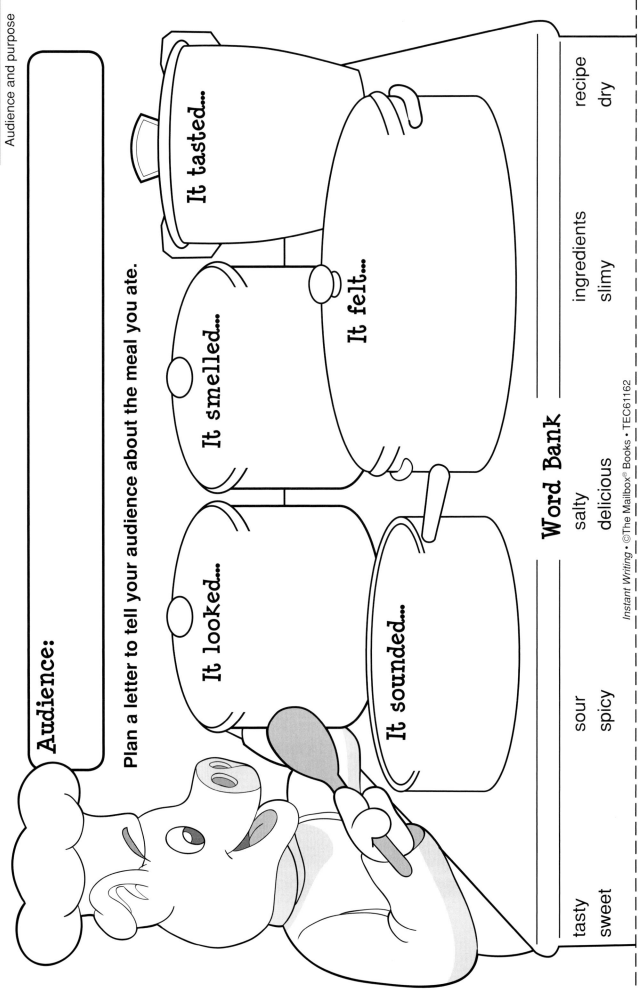

Audience:

Plan a letter to tell your audience about the meal you ate.

It looked...

It smelled...

It tasted...

It felt...

It sounded...

Word Bank

| tasty | sour | salty | ingredients | recipe |
| sweet | spicy | delicious | slimy | dry |

Instant Writing • ©The Mailbox® Books • TEC61162

Note to the teacher: Use with "What's Cooking?" on page 49.

A Surprise Visitor

Write a description about an unexpected guest. Read the word bank. Choose a main idea. Be sure to use lots of details that support your main idea.

Main Ideas

- The Dinosaur That Came to Visit

- The Drippy Pond Creature That Came to Visit

- The Storybook Character That Came to Visit

Word Bank

interesting
confused
amazed
stunned
gasped
smiled
screamed
well-dressed
scary
friendly

Descriptive writing

Main idea:

Write details to describe the unexpected guest.

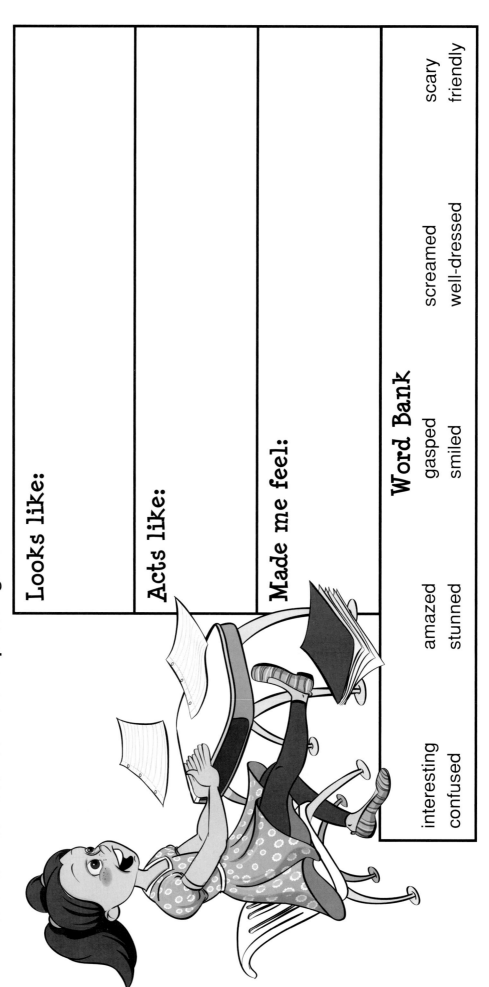

Looks like:

Acts like:

Made me feel:

Word Bank

interesting	amazed	gasped	screamed	scary
confused	stunned	smiled	well-dressed	friendly

Note to the teacher: Use with "A Surprise Visitor" on page 51.

Help Wanted

Write a job description.
Read the word bank. Choose a
    main idea.
Be sure to include details that
    describe the kind of person
    you would want to hire.

CLASSIFIEDS

Word Bank

special	searching
enjoy	perfect
need	money
fair	friendly
understand	dedicated

Main Ideas

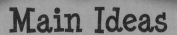

- Now hiring: a new friend

- Now hiring: a new neighbor

- Now hiring: a new sibling

- Now hiring: a new housekeeper

Descriptive writing

Descriptive writing

Main idea and details

Main idea:

Write details to describe the kind of person you would want to hire.

Personality description:	Job description:	Other important details:

carrot tester

Word Bank

| special | need | understand | perfect | friendly |
| enjoy | fair | searching | money | dedicated |

Note to the teacher: Use with "Help Wanted" on page 53.

Pets! Pets! Pets!

Write a descriptive paragraph about a pet.

Read the word bank. Choose a topic.

Be sure to include sensory details in your writing.

Topics

- The Silliest Pet
- An Unbelievable Pet
- The Perfect Pet

Word Bank

funny	playmate
obey	fur
boring	hairy
stinky	spotted
walk	noisy

PET SHOP OPEN

Name _____

Topic:

Plan a descriptive paragraph about a pet.

Looks like:

Sounds like:

Feels like:

Word Bank

| funny | boring | walk | fur | spotted |
| obey | stinky | playmate | hairy | noisy |

Note to the teacher: Use with "Pets! Pets! Pets!" on page 55.

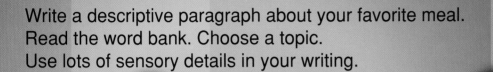

Now Serving

Write a descriptive paragraph about your favorite meal.
Read the word bank. Choose a topic.
Use lots of sensory details in your writing.

Word Bank

salty	creamy
sweet	crunchy
delicious	juicy
steamy	warm
sizzling	melted

Topics

- My Favorite Breakfast

- My Favorite Lunch

- My Favorite Dinner

Descriptive writing

Topic:

List details to help you plan a descriptive paragraph about your favorite meal.

Looks like:	Smells like:

Tastes like:	Sounds like:

Feels like:	

Word Bank

salty	delicious	sizzling	crunchy	warm
sweet	steamy	creamy	juicy	melted

Note to the teacher: Use with "Now Serving" on page 57.

A New Design

Write an advertisement to sell something you designed.
Read the word bank. Choose a topic.
Be sure to use sensory details in your ad.

Topics

- Kids Want This!
- Adults Want This!
- Teachers Want This!
- Animals Want This!

Word Bank

cool	popular	musical	busy
fun	bounces	learn	quiet
awesome			
educational			

Descriptive writing

Descriptive writing
Sensory details

Topic:

Plan an advertisement to sell your new design.

Draw your new design.

Looks like:

Smells like:

Feels like:

Sounds like:

Special features:

Word Bank

cool	awesome	popular	musical	busy
fun	educational	bounces	learn	quiet

Note to the teacher: Use with "A New Design" on page 59.

Special Delivery

Write a descriptive paragraph about what is inside the package.
Read the word bank. Choose a topic.
Be sure to use lots of adjectives in your writing.

Word Bank

quick	colorful
smooth	lazy
striped	shiny
huge	speckled
relaxing	

Topics

- Brand-New Bicycle
- Best Toy Ever
- Homework-Helper Machine
- The Most Incredible Skateboard

Topic: _____

Write several adjectives to plan a descriptive paragraph about what is inside the package.

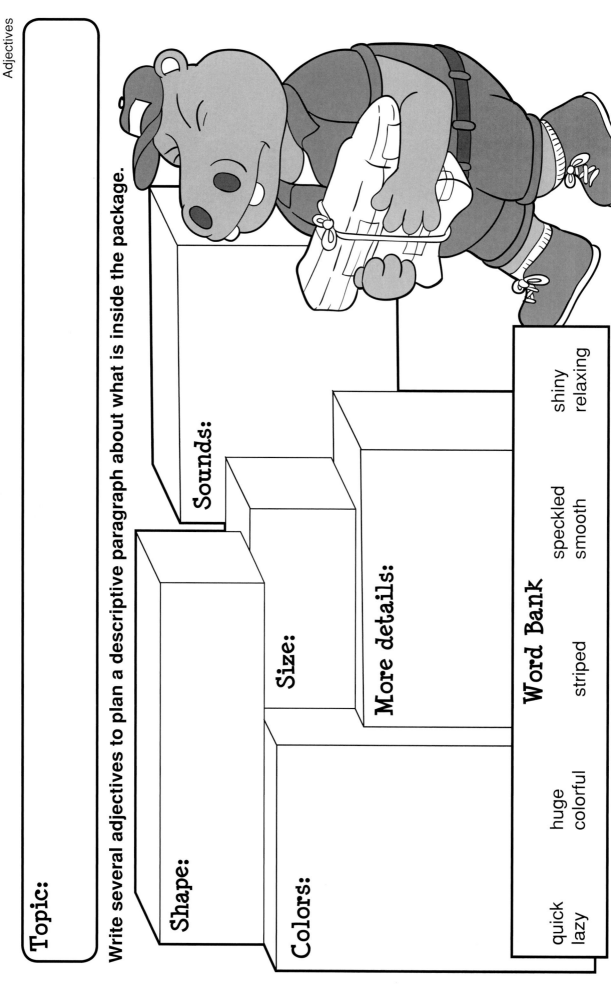

Shape:

Size:

Sounds:

Colors:

More details:

Word Bank

quick   huge   speckled   shiny

lazy   colorful   striped   smooth   relaxing

Instant Writing • ©The Mailbox® Books • TEC61162

Note to the teacher: Use with "Special Delivery" on page 61.

Wacky Weather

Write a poem about the weather.
Read the word bank. Choose a topic.
Make sure you use lots of adjectives in your poem.

Canada

United States of America

Word Bank

outside
forecast
drift
blow
change
sky
clouds
calm
peaceful
warning

Topics

- Snowstorm

- Rain showers

- Sunny days

- Fog

Descriptive writing

Name _____

64

Topic:

Write descriptive words and phrases to plan a poem.

Topic

Word Bank

outside	drift	change	clouds	peaceful
forecast	blow	sky	calm	warning

Instant Writing • ©The Mailbox® Books • TEC61162

Note to the teacher: Use with "Wacky Weather" on page 63.

Plant Problems

Write a letter to answer the worried gardener's question. Read the word bank. Choose a question.

Word Bank

patience	season	moist
flower	shade	saturated
soil	sunlight	temperature

Questions

- What does my plant need to help it grow?

- In October, all the leaves fell off my tree! What happened?

- I water my flowers five times every day, so why won't they grow?

- Why don't my carrot and potato plants have any vegetables on them?

Informational writing

Name_____

Question:

Write the facts about plants that will help you plan a
letter to answer the gardener's question.

Fact

Fact

Fact

Fact

Word Bank

patience	soil		sunlight	saturated
flower	season	shade	moist	temperature

Instant Writing • ©The Mailbox® Books • TEC61162

Ask the Pet Doctor!

Write an email in response to a customer's question.
Read the word bank. Choose a question.

Questions

- Why did my fuzzy caterpillar turn into a hard shell?

- Why did my snake shed its skin?

- Why does my fish flop around when I take it out of the water?

- If I get a pet, what will it need?

Word Bank

habit	popular	change	grow	breathe
learn	pleasant	life cycle	tight	habitat

Name _____

Question:

Write facts that will help you answer the customer's question.

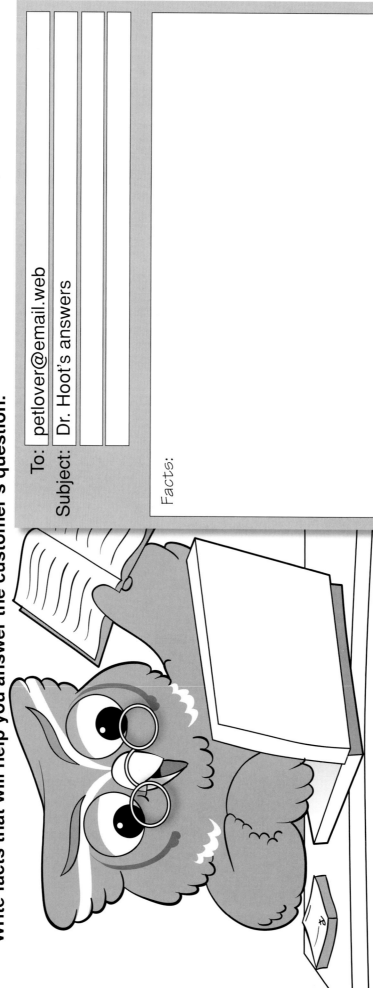

To: petlover@email.web

Subject: Dr. Hoot's answers

Facts:

Word Bank

habit	popular	change	grow
breathe	learn	pleasant	life cycle
	tight	habitat	

Instant Writing • ©The Mailbox® Books • TEC61162

Note to the teacher: Use with "Ask the Pet Doctor!" on page 69.

You're Invited!

Write an invitation to a party.
Read the word bank. Choose a topic.
Think about who the party is for, who to invite,
and what guests need to know.

Word Bank
friends
family
please
presents
surprise
exciting
house
bring
enjoy
afternoon

Topics
- Birthday Party
- Pool Party
- Costume Party
- Slumber Party

Invitation

Informational writing

Topic: _____

Plan the details for an invitation to a party.

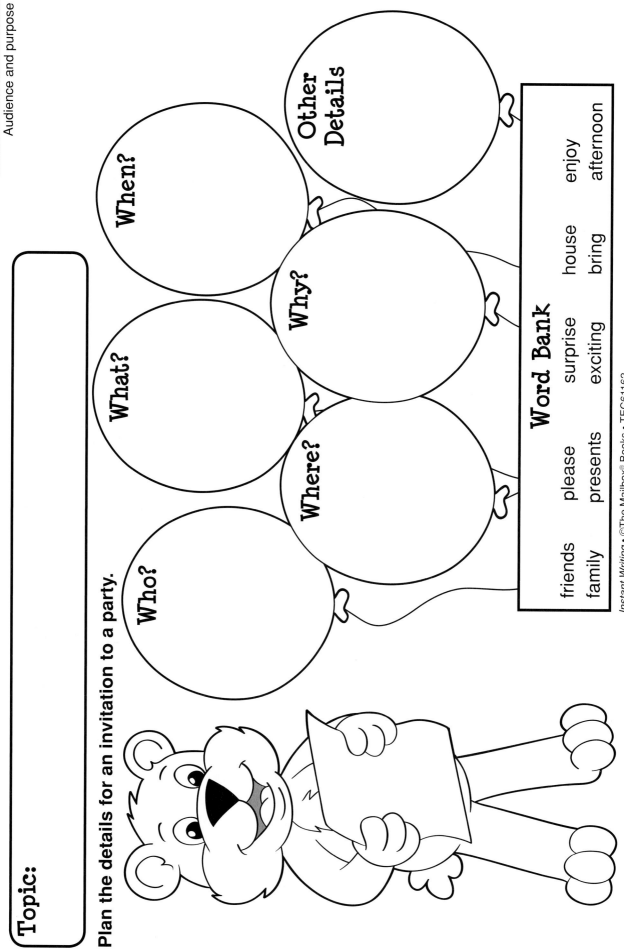

When?

Other
Details

What?

Why?

Who?

Where?

Word Bank

| friends | please | surprise | house | enjoy |
| family | presents | exciting | bring | afternoon |

Instant Writing • ©The Mailbox® Books • TEC61162

Safety First

Write an essay that explains safety rules.
Read the word bank. Choose a topic.
Think about what the safety rules are and why your readers should know them.

Topics

- Fire Safety

- Bicycle Safety

- Swimming Safety

- Playground Safety

Word Bank

protective gear
walk
quick
call
help
escape
plan
buddy
partners
careful

Informational writing

Informational Writing

Audience and purpose

Write important safety rules to plan an essay.

Topic: _____

Write a sentence to get your audience's attention.

✔ _____

What do you want your audience to know?

✔ _____

✔ _____

✔ _____

✔ _____

Word Bank

protective gear	quick	help	plan	partners
walk	call	escape	buddy	careful

Audience

Note to the teacher: Use with "Safety First" on page 71.

All Dressed Up

Write a paragraph that shares information about your wardrobe.
Read the word bank. Choose a main idea.
Be sure to include details that support your main idea.

Main Ideas
- Getting Dressed for School
- Getting Dressed for a Fancy Party
- Getting Dressed for a Sports Game

Word Bank

hand-me-down	tattered
brand-new	favorite
unusual	stylish
wear	popular
rags	plaid

Informational writing

Main idea:

Plan the details in your paragraph that support the main idea.

Detail:

Detail:

Detail:

Word Bank

hand-me-down	unusual	rags	favorite	popular
brand-new	wear	tattered	stylish	plaid

Pack Your Bags!

Write an essay about what you would pack on a selected trip.
Read the word bank. Choose a main idea.
Be sure to include details that support why you would pack such items.

Word Bank

suitcase
duffel bag
toothbrush
soap
damp
clothes
chilly
lotion
book
humid

Main Ideas

- A Trip to a Desert
- A Trip to the North Pole
- A Trip to a Beach
- A Trip to a Rain Forest

Informational writing

Main idea:

Plan the details for an essay that supports your main idea.

Need	Why?

Word Bank

suitcase	toothbrush	clothes	book	chilly
duffel bag	soap	lotion	damp	humid

Instant Writing • ©The Mailbox® Books • TEC61162

Note to the teacher: Use with "Pack Your Bags!" on page 75.

Fun and Games

Write directions for how to play a game. Read the word bank. Choose a topic. Be sure to think about the order of the steps in the directions.

Topics

- Pin the Tail on the Donkey

- Hide-and-Seek

- Musical Chairs

- Tag

Word Bank

outdoors	count
players	follow
listen	quick
turns	winner
fair	attempt

Topic: _____

Write the steps to plan the directions for a game.

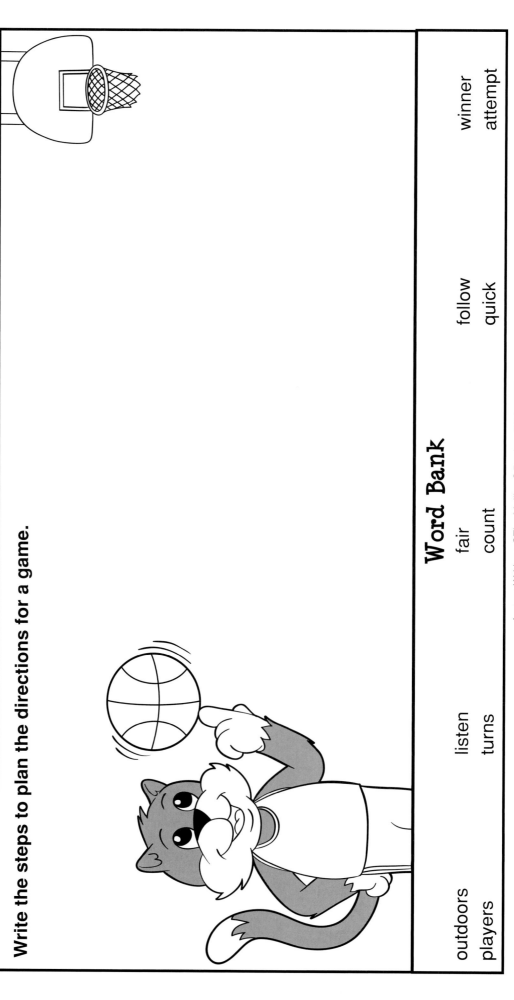

Word Bank

outdoors	listen	fair	follow	winner
players	turns	count	quick	attempt

Note to the teacher: Use with "Fun and Games" on page 77.

Scrub-a-dub-dub

Write directions for an activity.
Read the word bank. Choose a topic.
Be sure to think about the order of the steps
in the directions.

Topics

- Washing a Car
- Bathing a Pet
- Shampooing Hair
- Mopping a Floor

Word Bank

water
bubbles
lather
sponge
sudsy
slippery

rinse
splash
foam
towel

Informational writing

Name_____

Topic:

Write the steps to plan the directions for an activity.

Word Bank

water	lather	sudsy	rinse	foam
bubbles	sponge	slippery	splash	towel

Instant Writing • ©The Mailbox® Books • TEC61162

80   **Note to the teacher:** Use with "Scrub-a-dub-dub" on page 79.